Pinterest Perfect!

Creative prompts & pin-worthy projects inspired by the artistic community of **Pinterest**

www.walterfoster.com
3 Wrigley, Suite A
Irvine, CA 92618

Publisher: Rebecca J. Razo
Art Director: Shelley Baugh
Project Editor: Stephanie Meissner
Associate Editor: Jennifer Gaudet
Assistant Editor: Janessa Osle
Production Designers: Debbie Aiken, Amanda Tannen
Production Manager: Nicole Szawlowski
Production Coordinator: Lawrence Marquez

Printed in China.
1 3 5 7 9 10 8 6 4 2
18645

Pinterest Perfect!

Creative prompts & pin-worthy projects inspired by the artistic community of **Pinterest**

Flora Chang, Gemma Correll, Marisa Edghill, Khristian A. Howell, Molly Jacques, Jamielyn Nye, Ronda Palazzari & Amanda Wright

PINTEREST PERFECT!

Table of Contents

WATERCOLOR
Amanda Wright

MIXED MEDIA
Ronda Palazzari

ILLUSTRATION
Gemma Correll

DOODLING
Flora Chang

Introduction

With its pleasing aesthetic and focus on imagery, Pinterest™ is the perfect place to find creative inspiration! This popular social media platform has become more than just a place to collect—and swoon over—pretty pictures; it is a dynamic and interactive creative tool for artists, designers, illustrators, crafters, DIYers, hobbyists, and individuals who simply love beautiful things.

In **Pinterest Perfect!** you'll find 25 fun, easy-to-follow step-by-step projects and crafts, inspired by the artistic community of Pinterest. Ranging from mixed media, watercolor painting, and lettering to papercrafts, doodling, and illustration, each project includes simple instruction and beautiful images. With the guidance of the eight talented artists featured in this book, you will learn how to use simple materials to create pin-worthy works of art, gifts, stationery, and more. As an added bonus, you'll find helpful tips about effectively using Pinterest as an artist or hobbyist, including how to promote and market your work, as well as how to engage with and connect to likeminded folks, family and friends, and followers.

The creative journey doesn't end with the last page of this book, however. Along the way, you'll find open pages for sketching, brainstorming, collecting inspiration, and curating your own artistic endeavors. Throughout the book each artist offers tips and ideas for expanding projects and turning them into something more, allowing you to use **Pinterest Perfect!** as a catalyst for endless creativity.

So get your creative gears spinning…this is just the beginning!

Each project includes a list of the materials needed to complete it. Many projects only require a few materials that you may already have on hand, and others may spur you to expand your collection of art supplies. All of the required materials for the projects in this book can be found at your local arts & crafts store or favorite art supplies retailer.

Pinterest Perfect! is divided into eight sections: Papercrafts with Marisa Edghill, Crafts with Jamielyn Nye, Patterns with Khristian A. Howell, Hand Lettering with Molly Jacques, Watercolor with Amanda Wright, Mixed Media with Ronda Palazzari, Illustration with Gemma Correll, and Doodling with Flora Chang. Begin with the project that catches your attention first, and work your way through the book as inspiration strikes.

These projects are designed to engage and fuel your innate creative self. Feel free to experiment and explore! Allow your imagination to lead the way, guiding you to your own artistic expression. Use the open pages to practice techniques, sketch ideas, or paste photographs and swatches, creating your very own inspiration boards.

Be sure to check out the Artist Tips throughout the book for helpful hints or suggestions for tweaking the project to suit your needs. Make this book your own, and feel free to write in comments, ideas, or alternatives as you work!

Ready to start creating? Turn the page to get started!

PAPERCRAFTS
Marisa Edghill

CRAFTS
Jamielyn Nye

PATTERNS
Khristian A. Howell

HAND LETTERING
Molly Jacques

WATERCOLOR
Amanda Wright

MIXED MEDIA
Ronda Palazzari

ILLUSTRATION
Gemma Correll

DOODLING
Flora Chang

PAPERCRAFTS

Marisa Edghill

**ARTIST
PROFILE**

**KIRIGAMI
FLOWERS**

**PLEATED
BOWS**

**MINI PAPER
PINWHEELS**

**CUPCAKE
CARDS**

"One of my
favorite
things about
Pinterest is the
easy access
to international
inspiration."

Artist:
Marisa Edghill

I live and create in the small lakeside town of Midland, Ontario. I've lived in the country, in big cities, in the Caribbean, and in the Far East—now I'm trying small-town Canada on for size! My days are spent running a sweet online shop, Omiyage. I source each cute, clever, and crafty thing myself—tracking down wonderful goods from all over the world. There is something delightful about shipping orders both near and far, imagining what crafty adventures they're bound for.

Alongside the shop, I create DIY projects and tutorials. My work is strongly influenced by the time I spent living in Japan. Artisanal handiwork and attention to detail is found everywhere, and aesthetics stretch from *wabi sabi* to clean modernism to over-the-top cuteness. Plus there really is nothing better than to leisurely wander through a giant Japanese craft & hobby shop—unique products and handcrafted ideas abound!

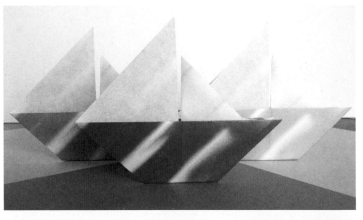

One of my favorite things about Pinterest is the easy access to international inspiration. As with fashion, so with craft, each country has its own trends and styles. Collecting inspiration has never been so easy! I love seeing how artists and bloggers around the world work with the same materials in different ways. As a resource, I use Pinterest to research ideas, compile inspiration files, and keep up to date on what's popular and what's next. It's also a wonderful place to share my own projects with others.

While I work most often with paper and tape, I am a self-professed dabbler. My creative messes aren't limited to papercraft—you might find me creating kirigami garlands one day and knitting a scarf the next. As the seasons change, so do my crafty pursuits. But, for now, why don't you grab some origami paper in your favorite shades, along with a handful of washi and glitter tape, and let's create something pin-worthy together.

 TO FIND OUT MORE

Visit **www.omiyage.ca** and **www.omiyageblogs.ca**. Connect with Marisa on Pinterest: **@OmiyageCA**.

PAPERCRAFTS
Marisa Edghill

Kirigami Flowers – Three Ways

Kirigami, from the Japanese *kiri* ("to cut") and *gami* ("paper"), is the art of cutting paper. For me, the joy of kirigami is taking something basic—a piece of paper— and transforming it into something beautiful with just a few folds and cuts. The secret to kirigami flowers is to make rounded cuts and create lots of negative space. You'll find templates for these three kirigami flowers on pages 26–27. You can use the templates as a reference while cutting freehand, or you can trace them onto your origami paper before cutting.

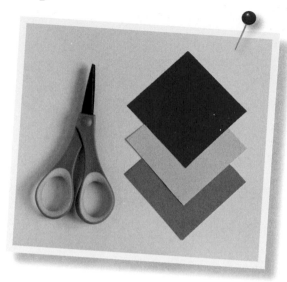

TOOLS & MATERIALS
3" (7.5cm) origami paper
Scissors
Bone folder (optional)

STEP 1 Fold a piece of origami paper in half diagonally.

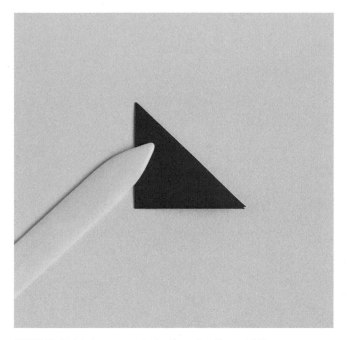

STEP 2 Fold the paper in half again. If you'd like, use a bone folder to sharply crease each fold. This step is optional, but it makes the folded paper easier to cut.

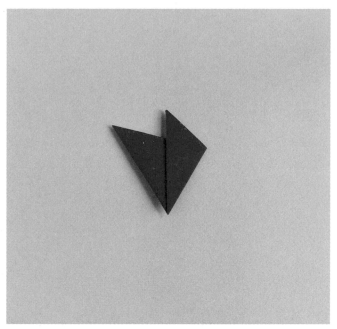

STEP 3 Turn the triangle so that the folded point is pointing toward you. Now the triangle needs to be folded into three equal parts. Fold the right third over the center third of the triangle and crease.

STEP 4 Flip the paper over and repeat. The edges should line up.

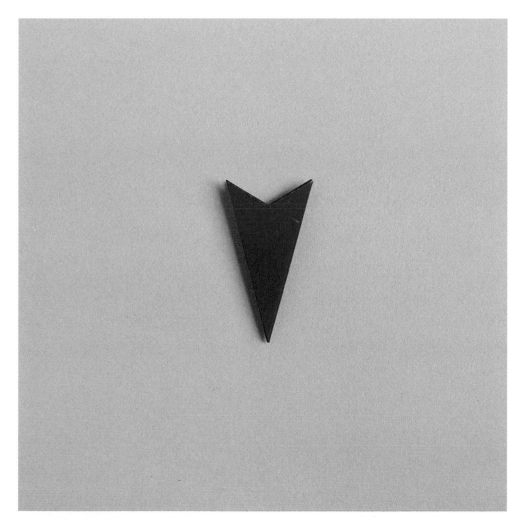

STEP 5 Cut straight across the top of the folded paper to remove the excess paper points.

STEP 6 Refer to the templates on pages 26–27 and choose the style of flower you would like to create. You can trace the template on your paper if you desire. Cut, being careful not to cut through the edges. I find it easiest to start at the top and work down.

ARTIST TIP

You have all these pretty paper flowers—now what? String your kirigami flowers onto a piece of twine or thin ribbon to create a garland. Perfect as a party decoration or to add a little personality to a blank wall!

STEP 7 Carefully unfold to reveal the kirigami flower. Flatten your paper flowers by placing them under a heavy book, or press gently with a dry iron on the lowest setting.

Pleated Bows

Beautiful giftwrapping abounds on Pinterest. From the simplest tag-and-paper combos to ornate piles of presents, there is inspiration for all occasions. In this project, learn how to craft a one-of-a-kind gift topper out of origami paper. Layering three different papers in pleated bows gives them a fun modern edge.

TOOLS & MATERIALS
6" (15cm) origami paper
Scissors or paper cutter
Washi tape

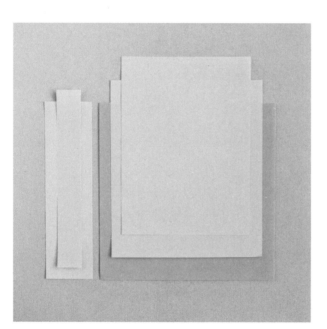

STEP 1 Select three sheets of origami paper in your desired colors or patterns. Decide the order you want them in. The bottommost piece of paper will be left whole. Cut a ¾" strip off the middle piece of paper and set the strip aside. This strip will be used to make the center of your bow. Cut a 1 ½" strip off the topmost piece of paper. You can use this strip to create mini paper pinwheels. (See pages 18-19.)

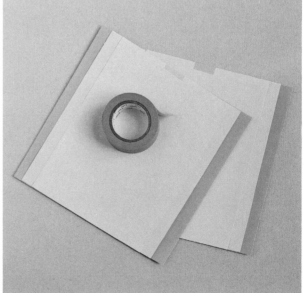

STEP 2 Layer the three sheets of paper on top of each other and secure on one side with a small piece of washi tape.

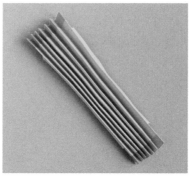

STEP 3 Holding the three pieces of paper together, fold the top ¼" of the layered edge backward. Crease firmly. Then make another ¼" fold, folding forward. Continue folding back and forth, creating clean accordion folds as you go until all of the paper is folded.

ARTIST TIP

Origami paper comes in a multitude of fun colors and patterns that are perfect for papercrafts. Don't feel limited to just making origami models; these thin yet strong papers are ideal for making all sorts of things, including bows, flowers, and more!

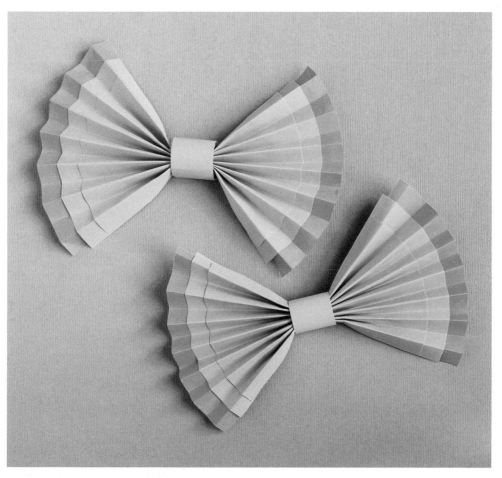

STEP 4 Holding the pleated paper in your hands, create the center of the bow by folding in half at the center. Unfold and fold again in the opposite direction. Unfold. If desired, you can remove the strip of washi tape. Loosely wrap the slim paper strip you cut off the middle layer of paper around the center of the bow. Secure with tape. Use your fingers to fan out the pleats into a bow.

Mini Paper Pinwheels

Mini paper pinwheels look adorable clustered together on top of a gift. You can use the paper strip cut from the top layer of your pleated bow. (See pages 16–17.) Want to skip the bows and jump right into making paper pinwheels? Start with a piece of origami paper (or other thin paper) cut to approximately 1 ½" – 2" wide by 6" long.

TOOLS & MATERIALS
Paper strips
Twine
Scissors
Glue
Glitter tape

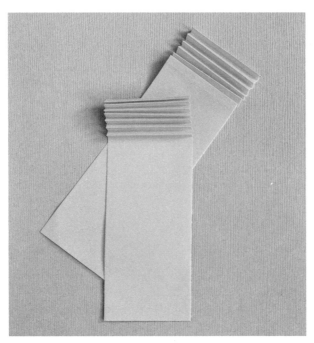

STEP 1 Fold the top edge of the paper strip backward. Your fold should be approximately ³⁄₁₆" wide. Then fold forward. Continue folding back and forth, making accordion folds, until the entire strip of paper is folded.

STEP 2 Tie a piece of twine around the center of the folded paper.

STEP 3 Fan out the pleats until the edges meet. Glue the loose edges together to form your pinwheel. Mini clothespins are perfect for keeping the edges together while they dry. Alternatively, you can simply press and hold them.

Washi tape makes a great ribbon substitute when wrapping gifts. Layer a couple different colors and patterns for more washi fun! For the finishing touch, top your gift with one of your pleated paper bows or a grouping of mini paper pinwheels.

STEP 4 Once the pinwheels are dry, add a focal point to hide the twine center. Cut a small circle out of glitter tape or a piece of thick paper. Adhere to the center of your pinwheels.

PAPERCRAFTS
Marisa Edghill

Washi Tape Cupcake Cards

Decadent treats, washi tape, and cute DIYs are always popular on Pinterest, so I couldn't resist combining them all into one sweet project. These cupcake cards are simple to make but still look impressive. They would be a wonderful way to invite friends over for an afternoon tea party.

One of my favorite ways to use washi tape is to create shaped cards like these. Multitasking washi tape is perfect for "coloring in" pictures and creating simple designs. Once you've mastered the cupcake, try expanding your repertoire to other shapes. If you can find it, glitter tape is a fantastic addition to your craft cupboard—all the fun of glitter, without the mess!

TOOLS & MATERIALS

8.5" x 11" cardstock

Scissors

Ruler

Washi tape

Glitter tape

Glue

Bone folder (optional)

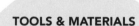

STEP 1 Fold the cardstock in half horizontally. For a clean fold use a bone folder. To create your card, cut off a 4" piece from the bottom of the folded cardstock and set aside. The folded edge will be the top of the card.

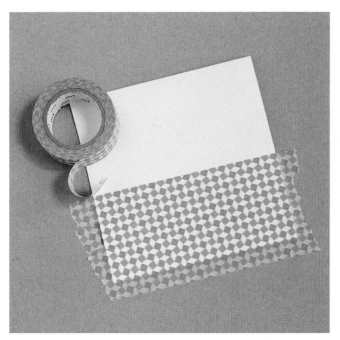

STEP 2 Place the card with the fold positioned at the top. Measure 2" up from the bottom of the card and make a small mark on each side. I use a bone folder to mark cards so there aren't pencil marks to erase. Apply strips of patterned washi tape to the card for the cupcake wrapper, working your way down from the marks until the bottom half is covered. Try to match up the pattern, if possible.

STEP 3 Trim the excess tape. At the bottom of the card, mark 1" in from each side. Cut a straight line from the bottom-right mark up to the middle mark you made in step 2. Repeat with the marks on the left side. If desired, round the bottom edges slightly.

STEP 4 Moving on to more delicious things, let's work on the icing. Mark the top edge at the center point of the card. Then mark a ¼" long horizontal line on each side of the center mark, approximately ³⁄₁₆" away from the center. The total width of your marked area should be about ³⁄₈". Then cover the top half of your card in strips of a solid color washi tape. Lay the first strip next to the top edge of your wrapper and work upward.

STEP 5 First cut a small connecting tab along the top folded edge, being careful not to cut off the back side of the card. Starting on one side, cut along the ¼" mark you made at the top of the card. Your markings should be visible through the translucent washi tape. Continue to cut, creating your desired icing shape, until you reach the point where the icing meets the wrapper. Repeat on the other side. I cut my cupcake top with a bit of wave to mimic swirls of icing, but you can also make a smooth dome.

STEP 6 Now it's time to decorate your card! Start by sticking a piece of glitter tape on a piece of cardstock. Cut a heart—or any other shape—out of the glitter tape. Glue the heart topper to the connecting tab at the top of the card.

STEP 7 To make sprinkles cut extra-thin strips of glitter tape in various colors; then snip into shorter lengths. Stick randomly on the icing. Add a sweet message inside, and your pin-worthy cupcake is ready to brighten someone's day!

Ideas & Inspiration

Use these pages to sketch out some ideas for your own kirigami flower templates or to collect origami paper and washi tape samples. Use the blank squares to "pin" paper and tape samples. Remember to write the name of the item or source in the gray box.

Kirigami Flower Templates

Use these templates to create the kirigami flowers shown on pages 12–15. You can photocopy them at any size you wish!

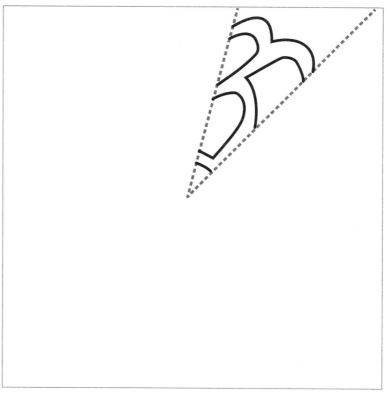

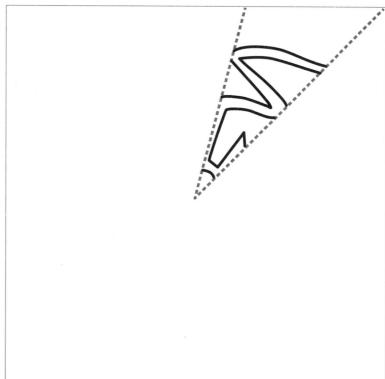

Building a Sense of Community

with Laurie Gatlin & Roy Reynolds

• As a form of social media, Pinterest is a great tool for building a sense of community amongst people with shared interests. First-year teachers, for example, tend to pin a lot of classroom-management tips. You can find others who share your interests by searching for pins or boards on topics that interest you. Peruse the myriad boards on Pinterest, and you'll find others who share your approach to a problem or project.

• As teachers, asking our students to follow us (and following them in return) allows us to see what they are individually working on. Asking students to follow one another enables them to share resources and get ideas from their peers. Use Pinterest to create and connect with groups of people that inspire and encourage you.

• There may come a time when you have to "unfollow" an individual, or some of their boards, because you just aren't interested in a topic—or their pins are flooding your feed. Pinterest does not notify pinners when they are unfollowed. Regularly updating and purging your lists keeps things fresh! Don't be afraid to unfollow.

Oh baby
it's a girl

CRAFTS

Jamielyn Nye

ARTIST PROFILE

GLITTER VASE

PAINTED CANVAS BAG

WHAT I LOVE MOST ABOUT MY HOME IS WHO I SHARE IT WITH

CLIPBOARD

" I truly believe that everyone has the ability to create beautiful things. "

Artist: Jamielyn Nye

My name is Jamielyn Nye, and I am the owner and founder of the creative lifestyle blog *I Heart Nap Time* and the creator of the online app, The Inspiration Board. I love to motivate women, get their creative juices flowing, and genuinely inspire.

I Heart Nap Time was born four years ago. With a drive and desire to create beauty in my life, cook delicious food for my darling hubby, and truly make a difference, I hit the ground running. My photographs tell stories and make it simple and easy for readers to begin creating. You'll find tutorials for DIY home projects on a budget, crafts, sewing, easy recipes, and tips and techniques. I work with a fabulous creative team to update the blog seven times a week, bringing readers

new content and inspiration. Every Saturday we host a weekly link party for readers to share their recent projects and ideas. With monthly views in the millions, *I Heart Nap Time* has become a hot commodity for those seeking a creative outlet all over the world. Our mission is to help others find the time to create by sharing tutorials, ideas, and support.

DIY chalk paint
and easy distressing technique

JELLO
cookies

I also write a weekly column for the *Baby Center* blog and have contributed on other sites, including *Mom it Forward*, *Tip Junkie*, and *Make and Takes*. My craft projects have been featured on many popular websites, including *Better Homes and Gardens*, *Martha Stewart*, *Fox*, *ABC*, *Examiner*, *Huffington Post*, *Parents*, and more.

I have always loved to create, ever since I was a little girl. I remember scrapbooking for hours on end, and I still have that creative passion and love to share it with others. I truly believe that everyone has the ability to create beautiful things.

When I'm not creating, I love to chase my two little monkeys and snuggle up on the couch with my man. I enjoy dreaming up delicious recipes, thrifting, and thinking of all the possibilities an old treasure can become.

 TO FIND OUT MORE
Visit **www.iheartnaptime.net**. Connect with Jamielyn on Pinterest: **@iheartnaptime**.

CRAFTS
Jamielyn Nye

Glitter Vase

Dress up an old mason jar with glitter to create a beautiful vase. You can customize this craft with different jars and colors to create a completely unique look!

TOOLS & MATERIALS
Mason jar
Double-sided tape
Glitter
Stencil brush

◄ **STEP 1** Clean your mason jar with warm water and soap. Allow the vase to dry. Place double-sided tape around the top of the jar.

► **STEP 2** Peel the backing from the tape and add glitter to it, using your stencil brush. Turn the jar around, and continue to apply the glitter to the tape.

STEP 3 Apply a few more rows of evenly spaced tape until you have reached the bottom of your jar. Continue to brush on the glitter until all of the tape is covered.

These vases make great centerpieces for any special occasion or day-to-day use. Make them as gifts or to decorate for your next party.

STEP 4 Dust off any excess glitter, and allow time to dry before using.

CRAFTS
Jamielyn Nye

Painted Canvas Bag

A personalized canvas bag is the perfect handmade gift. Paint polka dots, stripes, or a monogram with your choice of colored paint. Use these cute bags for gifts, party favors, or craft storage.

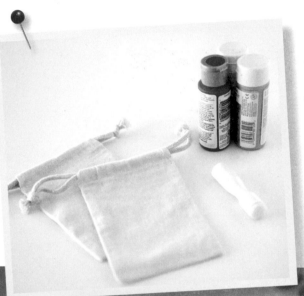

TOOLS & MATERIALS
Canvas or cotton bag
Acrylic paint
Dauber paintbrush
Small piece of paper
Brown paper bag

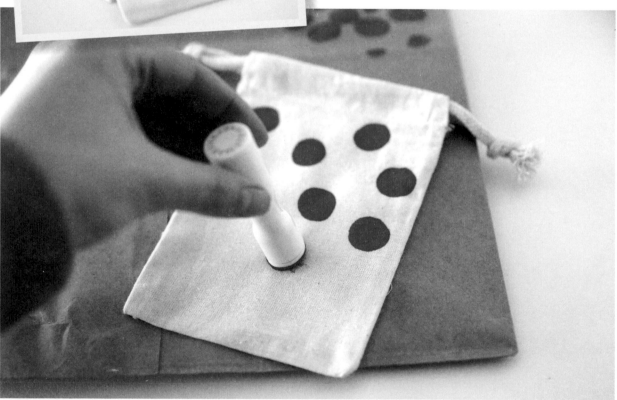

STEP 1 Gather your supplies and set them on a brown paper bag. Place a small piece of paper inside the bag to prevent the paint from bleeding onto your surface. Dab the paintbrush into the paint and lightly press the brush onto the bag.

STEP 2 Repeat until the bag is covered with your pattern. You can also use a stencil for this step. Remove the paper from inside the bag, and allow to dry.

STEP 3 Fill the bag with goodies, such as candy, soaps, or potpourri, and add a note if you're sending the bag as a gift!

PINTEREST TIP

Who's Pinning YOU?

with Laurie Gatlin & Roy Reynolds

If you have a blog or website, you can do a simple search to see if people have pinned items from them. Type the following into the address bar in your browser: www.pinterest.com/source/yourwebsite.com. You don't need "http://" or "www." before your website or blog address—just the name of your site and ".com" or your blog address. You'll see what items are popular among readers, and you can see how often an item has been re-pinned. Want to build a bigger community? Follow those who have pinned images from your blog!

CRAFTS
Jamielyn Nye

Clipboard

Create a custom wooden clipboard on which to hang all of your favorite quotes and pictures. Make it unique with different colors and sizes of stripes.

TOOLS & MATERIALS

12" x 10" wooden board

120-grit sandpaper

Paintbrush

Paint (2 colors)

Painter's tape or artist tape

Metal clip

E-6000 glue

STEP 1 Prep your board by sanding down the edges, and then wipe it clean. Paint the board one solid color and allow it to dry. You may need two coats of paint for your base color.

For even stripes, place an extra piece of tape between each strip to ensure your spacing is even. Then remove the extra pieces before you begin painting.

STEP 2 Create stripes on top of your board with painter's tape or artist tape. Leave about 1" between each piece of tape. Then paint between the tape with your second color to create the stripes. Allow the paint to dry; then carefully peel off the tape.

STEP 3 Adhere the metal clip at the top of the board with E-6000 glue, and your board is ready to display your favorite photos or pieces of art.

Ideas & Inspiration

Create an inspirational style board! Use these pages to draw, sketch, doodle, brainstorm, and paste photos, ideas, and concepts for other craft projects. Use magazines, blogs, Pinterest, and your imagination to curate a collection of ideas to spark your imagination and fuel your inner artist.

Khristian A. Howell

**ARTIST
PROFILE**

**EASY PATTERNED
GIFT WRAP**

**FESTIVE COCKTAIL
NAPKINS**

**GLAM
PLACE MATS**

" I deeply believe in living
a life that is colorful,
balanced, and inspired. "

Artist:
Khristian A. Howell

Well hey ya'll! I have to start this fun insight into my world with my number one truth of the moment: I am a southern girl living in an arctic world! My current center of gravity is the magical city of Chicago; however, in the next moment you may find me in Atlanta, New York, Miami, or abroad. This traveling life is par for the course when you are married to a newsman. I can work from anywhere, thus supporting my husband's dream while nurturing my own. This is what makes me so thrilled and thankful about what I am privileged to do for a living. I hope that my passion for travel and living a life inspired is evident in all my work. I deeply believe in living a life that is colorful, balanced, and inspired.

I am Khristian A. Howell, a color and pattern expert, and under my brand—Khristian A. Howell Color + Pattern—I license my work to large and small manufacturers; consult on trend, color, and design; and lend my voice as a color expert and lifestyle consultant. My work has been featured in *ELLE DECOR, Real Simple, HGTV Magazine,* and more. I am also a frequent contributor to *Better Homes and Gardens* magazine.

If your reaction is "Huh?" (not uncommon), I'll answer some questions that usually follow.

Question: Sooo, you're like an interior designer?

Answer: Yes…that is a part of my business. The bread and butter of my business is licensing. I lend the right for manufacturers to reproduce my artwork on their products. I work in a wide range of categories, from stationery to home décor to tech accessories. I also maintain an online shop full of colorful goodies that are a combination of product created in the studio and licensed product. I also consult for companies and private clients on color, pattern, and space. I assist companies with color and industry trends to keep their products cutting-edge and fresh, and I work with private clients to help them transform their spaces—purely using the power of color and pattern.

Question: How did you get into that? Did you study art?

Answer: When I met my husband, I found myself in Seattle because of his work. In my eyes, the only game in town was to work at Nordstrom headquarters. I had no art degree. Armed with my degree in advertising, and what I believed to be an innate design sense, I landed a job as a colorist in kidswear product development. Luckily I sat with all the artists, and I wanted to know what they were up to. I started asking a lot of questions. Soon I began helping with simple tasks, such as recoloring artwork. I started creating artwork and offering it to the team to help with their large workload. Together we created artwork for kidswear for boys and girls, from babies to tweens. The rest, as they say, is history! This experience helped me gain confidence, as well as to understand the business of making designs come to life.

That is me in a nutshell. When I am not working hard at growing my business, you can find me on my yoga mat or dreaming about the olive grove I will tend to in my next life in Provence!

à bientôt!

 TO FIND OUT MORE

Visit **www.khristianahowell.com**. Connect with Khristian on Pinterest: **@KhristianHowell**.

43

Easy Patterned Gift Wrap

I love nothing more than a beautifully wrapped gift! This easy project is a great way to add a little color and pattern to any paper you have lying around. Kraft paper works great because it is very sturdy, but any paper will do!

TOOLS & MATERIALS
Kraft paper
Artist tape
Spray paint
Scissors
Drop cloth

STEP 1 Tape your desired pattern on a large sheet of kraft paper. Stripes look good and are easy. Try varying the size and angle for a more interesting effect. You could also create a grid pattern using straight lines or intersecting triangles. Don't press too firmly; you want to be able to easily remove the tape without tearing the paper.

 **ARTIST TIP**

Try this idea using the tissue paper that often comes with shopping bags. Instead of using tape to create a pattern, use a simple shape made of cardstock, such as a star, heart, dot, or rosette. Lay the cardstock pieces down in your desired pattern and apply spray paint from a good distance (2 feet). The result is your pattern in the negative space. So pretty! Vary the size of your cardstock patterns for a truly unique, pattern-ful effect! Now you have pretty tissue for gift bags.

ARTIST TIP

High-contrast colors look best on the kraft paper; however, gold and silver are gorgeous for a more festive look for holidays and weddings. You can also use black or white for high impact and embellish with colorful washi tape and ribbon!

STEP 2 Spray! Apply the spray paint in light layers. The drying time will be quick when applied lightly. Give the paper a good 10–15 minutes to dry.

STEP 3 Carefully remove the tape at an angle to prevent tearing. Ta-da! With just a few easy steps you have fun, graphic gift wrap made from items you likely have at home.

Festive Cocktail Napkins

It may be the New Orleans girl in me, but I love nothing more than throwing a gorgeous candlelight-filled cocktail party! I adore making a party pretty down to the smallest details, and I want my guests to feel pampered, comfortable, and special in my home.

I always seem to have leftover plain cocktail napkins from a party or the holidays. Adding a little pop of pattern to your bar cart can be quite nice! Try this easy little trick the next time you are ready to pop some bubbly with friends.

Note: This project is for decorative purposes only.

TOOLS & MATERIALS

Plain white napkins

Spray paint

Stencil of choice

Artist tape

STEP 1 Gently secure the napkin on or inside your stencil with artist tape. It is nice to open up the napkin one fold so the pattern continues over both sides.

 **ARTIST TIP**

I love using this pretty little pot as a stencil. Using something rounded like this is perfect for this project, plus I love the lacey look it creates!

STEP 2 Spray lightly with spray paint. You don't want the napkin to get too wet, and you don't want the look to be splotchy. You just want a hint of pattern and texture.

ARTIST TIP

Don't want everything to look one note? Create a set with different print ideas. Perhaps one allover pattern, one with a light ombre effect, and another with a large icon going off the edge, such as a piece of a large star on the corner. Play with different motifs and patterns!

STEP 3 Allow the napkin to dry for a bit in or under the stencil. It only takes a few minutes if applied lightly. Voilà! Unique decorative napkins, handcrafted by you!

PATTERNS
Khristian A. Howell

Glam Place Mats

Want to get the whole family excited about sitting down for dinner? Make the table a destination. This project allows you to easily update your tablescapes without breaking the bank. You can find inexpensive, plain fabric place mats just about anywhere. Better yet, recycle old place mats by flipping them over and starting fresh on the back!

Block printing has been around for centuries, and it is one of the easiest ways to create patterns out of your favorite shapes. You can even carve your own stamps for block printing from wood or rubber.

TOOLS & MATERIALS
Plain fabric place mats
Fabric paint
Paintbrush
Stamp of choice

STEP 1 Prep your stamp. I chose wooden circles and "T" shapes for my stamp. Adding a thumbtack as a little handle makes it easier to lift the stamp cleanly.

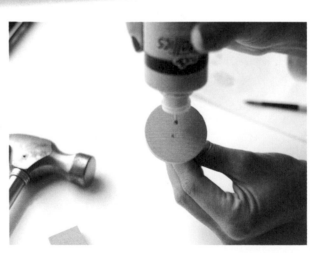

STEP 2 Apply a light coat of fabric paint directly to the stamp. This gold paint has an easy applicator, but you can brush the paint on as well. Don't apply the paint all the way to the edge of the stamp or it will ooze out when you stamp it. With a simple shape like these circles, you can always add more paint by stamping over the area again.

STEP 3 Stamp! Give it a firm push.

STEP 4 Hold the fabric firmly in place when you pull up the stamp. This ensures that the stamp pulls up cleanly, leaving a nice shape behind.

STEP 5 Keep going to complete your desired pattern.

STEP 6 As you move on to the other place mats, create your own collection and play with pattern mixing. I like the items on my table to work together but not necessarily match. Mix and match by using different stamps. Have fun playing! Follow the instructions on your fabric paint for setting the paint and washing.

Try Stripes!

STEP 1 Tape thin pieces of cardboard in place with artist tape to create a stripe.

ARTIST TIP

Creating patterns that work seamlessly together is all about balance. If you create one pattern that is very dense, create another that has more negative space. Mixing large-scale motifs with small-scale motifs also helps create a collection that works together beautifully.

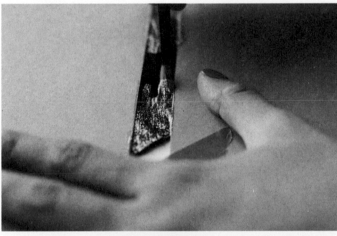

STEP 2 Use a small paintbrush to paint between the pieces of cardboard.

STEP 3 Vary the thickness of the stripes for interest, or keep them uniform. You can paint stripes across the whole place mat, or just a section. The sky is the limit!

Pattern Inspiration

Use these blank squares to "pin" interesting or pretty patterns from magazines, advertisements, or even Pinterest! Remember to write the name of the pattern or source in the gray box. When you need a little creative spark, perusing your favorite patterns may give your imagination just what it needs to generate a new idea.

You can't Do it All

Thank You

i feel that there is nothing more truly artistic than to love people. Vincent Van Gogh

HAND LETTERING

Molly Jacques

**ARTIST
PROFILE**

**LAVENDER
PLACE CARDS**

**PERPETUAL
CHALKBOARD
CALENDAR**

**CHALKBOARD
ANNOUNCEMENT**

> I'm an immense fan of
> DIY projects and teaching my
> friends and family how
> to make anything beautifully
> adorned with lettering.

Artist: Molly Jacques

I'm Molly, a typographical artist with a strong emphasis on calligraphy and hand lettering. I like to work on a wide array of projects, including typeface design, editorial hand lettering, illustration, and wedding calligraphy. It's been an honor to have some of my work featured in publications such as *Communication Arts*, *HOW*, *Martha Stewart Weddings*, and *Every Day with Rachael Ray*. My signature style is bold, modern lettering paired with traditional corporate calligraphy and illustrative elements. I keep my work minimalistic in color and honor innovation and movement.

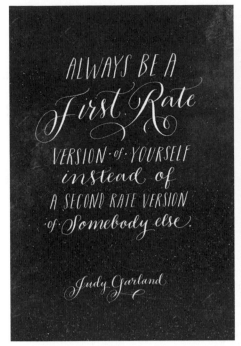

With great encouragement from my parents, I grew up knowing that I wanted to pursue an artist's life after school, and I studied illustration and design in college. After receiving my BFA from College of Creative Studies in Detroit, Michigan, my husband and I moved to Los Angeles to pursue our ideal careers and enjoy the sunshine. It didn't take long for me to realize that my heart was always in Michigan, and now we're back in Detroit, where I work from home as a fulltime, freelance lettering artist.

When I'm not in my studio, I enjoy backpacking, hiking, a good cup of coffee, and hanging out with my husband, Cody, and our two dogs, Fieval and Dakota. Even when I'm not working in my studio, I love to take my calligraphy pen and ink and help out with family projects and weddings, lending my creativity to those I love most. I'm an immense fan of DIY projects and teaching my friends and family how to make anything beautifully adorned with lettering.

 TO FIND OUT MORE

Visit **www.mollyjacquesillustration.com**. Connect with Molly on Pinterest: **@mollyjacques**.

Lavender Place Cards

Next time you have a dinner party or special event, try making these simple, yet elegant, place cards for your guests.

TOOLS & MATERIALS
Hole punch
Scissors
8" x 10" kraft paper
(or pre-cut kraft cards)
White jelly roller pen
White twine
Sprigs of lavender

STEP 1 Start by cutting out the shape of the place card with your scissors. I like my card to be small enough that it doesn't throw off the balance of the piece as a whole. Typically 1 ½" x 3" works well for place cards.

STEP 2 Once you've found a shape that you like for the card, use a small hole punch to punch a hole on one end of the card. This is where your card will attach to the lavender.

STEP 3 Cut 5" to 6" of white twine and loop it through the punched hole in your place card. I like to cut a little extra, just in case I want to double-wrap the twine around the lavender sprigs.

STEP 4 Use a white jelly roller pen to write the names of your guests on each place card. When I write names with my pen, I like to give them a "calligraphy" feel by adding extra line weight where each down stroke occurs. Have fun with this part! You can even use a variety of styles with your lettering, mixing and matching cards to create an overall texture of names.

STEP 5 Loop the twine attached to your place card around the lavender sprigs and secure with a knot. I loop around a few times to create a crisscrossing effect and secure with a bow. Once the card is secured, cut off any extra twine on the ends of your bow.

HAND LETTERING
Molly Jacques

Perpetual Chalkboard Calendar

Make this chalkboard calendar for a cute addition to any wall in your home. There's no need to replace it each year. The grid and days of the week always stay in place. Just erase and update the month and day numbers each month.

TOOLS & MATERIALS
White charcoal pencil
Ruler
12" x 18" Chalkboard

STEP 1 Start by using your white charcoal pencil and ruler to section the chalkboard into a grid for the calendar days. Draw seven rows across the board, starting at the bottom. I like to make marks on the bottom row for where my next set of grid lines will go. Use the ruler to draw straight lines for seven columns. Make sure you leave room at the top to write the days of the week and the name of the month.

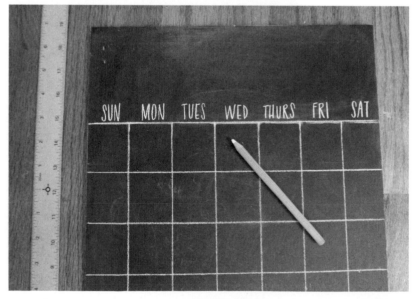

STEP 2 Write the days of the week across the top of your grid. Each day should fit over a single square and should read graphically. For my weekday lettering, I used an easy, legible hand. You can experiment with styles of writing.

STEP 3 Write the name of the month and the year at the top of the chalkboard. I used a script font to contrast with the lettering I used to write the days of the week. You can imitate my writing here, or you can explore other styles and create something of your own!

STEP 4 Next fill in the dates with the charcoal pencil, writing each number in the upper left-hand corner of each grid square. Be sure to refer to a finished calendar for reference!

STEP 5 Your calendar is finished! Find a spot to display it in your home and show off your hard work. Use your charcoal pencil to add appointments or special events.

HAND LETTERING
Molly Jacques

Chalkboard Announcement

A simple chalkboard with pretty script is the perfect photo prop for special events, announcements, and invitations. You can customize this for just about any news you wish to share with friends and family. I work with a lot of mothers-to-be and brides, so I chose "And Baby Makes 3" for my chalkboard.

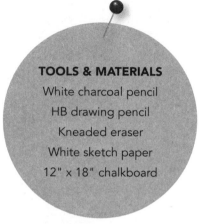

TOOLS & MATERIALS
White charcoal pencil
HB drawing pencil
Kneaded eraser
White sketch paper
12" x 18" chalkboard

STEP 1 Start by drawing small sketches with the HB pencil on your white sketch paper, brainstorming the words you'd like to announce. Do your best to work to scale of your chalkboard, or you can do small thumbnail sketches like mine.

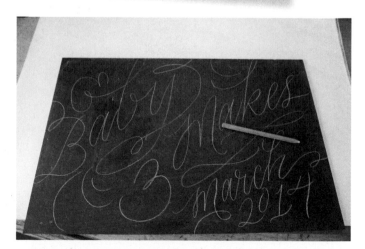

STEP 2 Once you have chosen your wording and a working design, freehand a rough version of your lettering onto your chalkboard, using the white charcoal pencil. At this stage, I write all my words in one line weight to help gauge the general placement.

STEP 3 With your general lettering in place, go back in and add smaller details, such as line weight. I drew in the perimeters for line weight on my script lettering, marking thicker lines for all the downstrokes of the style.

ARTIST TIP

Here are some other ideas for using a chalkboard announcement:

- Birthdays
  Example: Will is 2!

- Weddings
  Example: Just hitched!

- Holidays
  Example: Seasons Greetings from our family to yours.

- Engagements
  Example: Save the Date!

- Graduations
  Example: Rachel—Class of 2015

STEP 4 Fill in the negative areas of your lettering. I like my lettering to look solid, so I colored in all of the perimeters for line weight of the script with my charcoal pencil. The charcoal pencil is great for this because it can handle small details. Add in any illustrative elements you desire.

STEP 5 Use your newly drawn chalkboard as a prop for photos to announce your big news! If you have a professional photographer shooting your wedding, engagement session, or pregnancy, take your sign along to the shoot and let them know you'd like to use it.

Ideas & Inspiration

Create an inspirational style board! Use these pages for lettering practice and to brainstorm and collect photos, ideas, and concepts for original hand-lettered art.

Secret Boards

with Laurie Gatlin & Roy Reynolds

The ability to create a board that remains private has a lot of great applications. Secret boards are not available to the public and are great for teachers, planning a surprise party or wedding, or creating a gift wish list.

Amanda Wright

**ARTIST
PROFILE**

**PIXEL
PAINTING**

**TAPE
PAINTING**

**PAINTED
GREETING CARDS**

> " I try to squeeze a little creativity into every aspect of my life. I'm happiest when I'm making things."

Artist: Amanda Wright

I'm Amanda. I live in Cary, North Carolina, in a funny little A-frame house with my husband, two dogs, and an outrageous number of houseplants. I run my shop, Wit & Whistle, from my studio in our basement. Wit & Whistle offers witty greeting cards and whistle-worthy paper and home goods—all designed and illustrated by me.

I started my own business because my old job as a graphic designer didn't allow me the creative freedom I hoped for. Designing websites, logos, and such required some creativity, but it wasn't the frivolous sort of creativity that Wit & Whistle allows me to indulge in. I feel so blessed to be able to do what I love. Every night I lie in bed with endless ideas and possibilities floating around in my head, and every morning I'm excited to hop out of bed and get to work.

My designs begin as pen-and-ink drawings in my sketchbook. I often have to work around my two dogs (who prefer to be curled up in my lap at all times), which really adds to the creative challenge. Many of my greeting card designs have been inspired by laughter-filled conversations with friends, and my infatuation with interior design has led me to craft a variety of textile-inspired patterns.

I never limit myself to one creative outlet, and this helps keep my creative juices flowing. I have a background in fine art, and I love painting and sketching just for fun. I also dream up DIY projects, decorate my home, play in the garden, hone my photography skills, and experiment with new recipes. In short, I try to squeeze a little creativity into every aspect of my life. I'm happiest when I'm making things!

 TO FIND OUT MORE

Visit **www.witandwhistle.com**. Connect with Amanda on Pinterest: **@witandwhistle**.

WATERCOLOR
Amanda Wright

Pixel Painting

TOOLS & MATERIALS
Digital photograph
Photo-editing software (such as
Adobe Photoshop®)
Watercolor paper (one sheet)
Pencil • Ruler
Watercolor paintbrush
Watercolor paints
Paint palette
Cup of clean water
Paper towel

These watercolor pixel paintings are a bit time consuming, but the simple task of painting each square a different color is almost Zenlike. The painting process is a great way to hone your color-mixing skills, and the finished piece makes a wonderful personalized gift.

STEP 1 Choose a digital photograph from which to work. Landscapes work very well for pixel paintings, since they are recognizable even in their most simplified form. Open the photograph in your photo-editing software, and resize it to 16-pixels wide. Zoom in until the shrunken photograph takes up the whole screen and you can see each individual pixel. Crop the image down to 20-pixels high. Resize several different photographs until you find the one that looks best when pixelated.

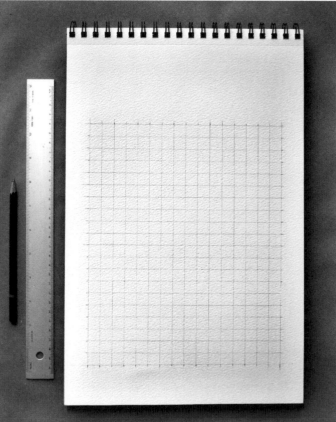

STEP 2 Measure an 8" x 10" rectangle on your paper, and lightly pencil in a grid. Be sure to use paper specifically made for use with watercolors, which can be purchased from your local arts & crafts store. Make each grid square ½" tall by ½" wide. Your finished grid should be 16 squares across and 20 squares down—the same number of pixels in your pixelated photograph.

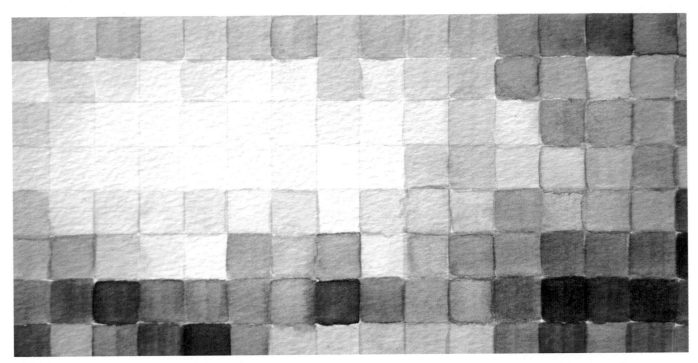

STEP 3 Grab your watercolors and begin painting one square at a time. Try to paint each square on your paper the same color as the corresponding pixel in your photograph. The colors don't have to match exactly—loosen up and have fun with it! To prevent the color from one square bleeding into a neighboring square, allow a little drying time and don't paint adjacent squares one after the other. Try painting every other square, and when you reach the end of the row go back and paint the squares you skipped.

STEP 4 Keep painting until you have filled all the squares. If you make a mistake, simply dab the wet paint with a dry paper towel to remove it. Watercolors are very forgiving.

STEP 5 Allow your painting to completely dry once all the squares are filled in. Your beautiful painting is ready to slip into a standard 8" x 10" frame!

Tape Painting

This project is perfect, whether you're a watercolor beginner or an old pro. The finished painting has a stained-glass look, and the colors are easily customizable to coordinate with any color palette. There's no better way to fill that empty spot on your wall than with a gorgeous painting you made yourself!

TOOLS & MATERIALS
Watercolor paper (one sheet)
¼" wide masking tape
Watercolor paintbrush
Paint palette
Watercolor paints
Cup of clean water
Paper towel

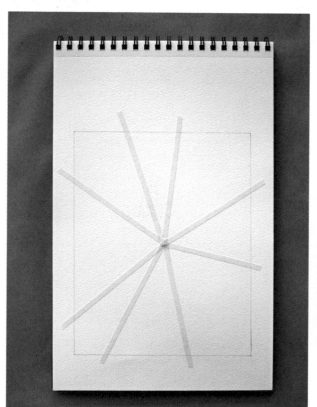

STEP 1 Use a ruler to draw an 8" x 10" rectangle on your paper. Then apply ¼" masking tape in a radial pattern outward from the center of your paper. Be sure to use paper specifically made for watercolors.

STEP 2 Add more tape to divide the large segments into smaller fragments until you have a balanced radial design.

ARTIST TIP

Other types of paint require the addition of white pigment to lighten colors, but with watercolors you just add more water to lighten the shade. Water increases the paint's transparency and allows the white of the paper to show through. The more water you use the lighter your color will be. If you haven't used watercolors before, practice painting gradients (see step 4) on a scrap of paper before beginning your tape painting.

STEP 3 Decide what colors you want to use in your painting. You can use as many or as few colors as you'd like. For this project it's easiest to mix up a good-sized puddle of each color before you begin painting. You want the paint you mix to be fairly pigmented—concentrated and not too watery.

STEP 4 Next paint a gradient in each taped-off segment. Dip your brush in the paint, and brush it onto the first quarter of a taped-off section. Then dip your brush in clean water to lighten the color and paint the next quarter, overlapping a bit with the first area you painted. Continue to dip your brush in clean water every so often as you paint further along the segment. This makes the color lighter and lighter as you go, creating a smooth gradient. You can dab up any mistakes with a dry paper towel.

STEP 5 Repeat step 4 for each taped-off fragment. Intersperse different paint colors around the painting as you go until your painting is complete.

STEP 6 Once the paint is dry, peel the masking tape off of the paper very slowly and carefully. If you pull too quickly the top layer of paper may peel up with it. Don't despair if, despite your best efforts, the paper starts to pull up with the tape. To repair the damage, put a tiny smudge of glue on the back of the peeled up paper and press it back down.

STEP 7 When all the tape is peeled off, your painting is complete and ready to hang or frame. Stand back and admire your handiwork!

Painted Greeting Cards

Letter writing has become a lost art these days, but e-mail can't compete with the charm of receiving a handwritten note in the mail. If you really want to wow your friends and family, try painting your own one-of-a-kind greeting cards to send out.

TOOLS & MATERIALS

Watercolor-paper note cards
(with envelopes)
Liquid frisket (available at art
supply stores)
Old paintbrush
Watercolor paintbrush
Paint palette
Watercolor paints
Cup of clean water

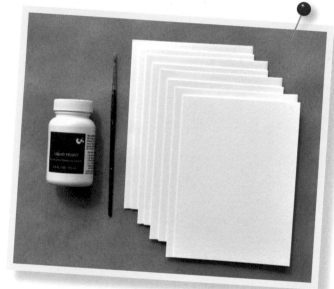

STEP 1 Use an old paintbrush (one you don't mind ruining) to paint liquid frisket on blank watercolor-paper note cards. Paint a different pattern or message on the front of each card. If you make a mistake, just let the frisket dry; it will peel right off the paper so you can try again. The frisket will act as a mask, and areas painted with it will remain white and paint-free when you apply paint. After you've perfected your designs, set the cards aside and let the frisket dry.

STEP 2 Once dry, you can paint right over the frisket with your watercolors. Paint splashes of color over the front of each card. Then let the paint dry completely.

ARTIST TIP

After you've painted the cards, why not add a little color to the envelopes as well? When you're ready to send a card, paint the recipient's address right onto the envelope for a beautiful finishing touch.

STEP 3 Now the fun part! Rub the frisket with your fingertip. It will ball up, and you'll be able to peel it off the paper. Your design will be revealed in crisp white, surrounded by a wash of watercolor.

STEP 4 Remove the frisket from all the cards, and your hand-painted cards are ready to send to friends and family!

Ideas & Inspiration

Create an inspirational style board! Use these pages to draw, sketch, doodle, brainstorm, and paste photos, ideas, and concepts for original pin-worthy painting projects. Use magazines, blogs, Pinterest, and your imagination to curate a collection of ideas to spark your imagination and fuel your inner artist.

Investigating Pins

with Laurie Gatlin & Roy Reynolds

Food is the number one item pinned on Pinterest, followed closely by Arts & Crafts; however, not all of these pins lead to reliable sources. One way to check the veracity of a pin is to click through and read comments on the original post. You may find comments such as, "Pinned this! It looks great!" However, keep looking until you find responses from those who have actually tried the recipe or project; they often give hints on difficult aspects or substitutions that may have been successful or unsuccessful.

Clicking through and reading the instructions can also reveal if someone has mislabeled a pin as a project or tutorial, when in fact, the link leads to a different type of website. Anyone can add comments to a pin, and simply re-pinning without taking a moment to investigate multiplies misidentified pins. Do your part in keeping quality of pins high for your followers.

 **Mixed Media**

Ronda Palazzari

ARTIST PROFILE

PONDER BIRD CANVAS

MISS FRANCES COLLAGE

TANGLED HEART

> " I love documenting emotions and everyday moments through art, art journals, and scrapbook pages. "

Artist: Ronda Palazzari

My name is Ronda, like the Beach Boys song, "Help Me Rhonda," only no "h." Art has been my voice since I was just a little kid finger painting and drawing. I started college as an art major and thought to myself, "What am I going to do with an art degree?" So I switched to elementary education. Who knew that later in life I would be able to marry both career goals?

I am a mixed media artist, author, licensed designer, instructor, and avid memory keeper. I enjoy all kinds of mediums, documenting stories, taking photographs, and compiling it all together into cohesive art pieces.

I like to call my style "Uptown Antique Brie"—a little class, a little vintage, and a lot of good cheese. I love new, flashy stuff but have an appreciation for vintage items. Playing it safe has never been my style, so you will find me pushing the envelope and using products in unexpected ways.

I am a color junkie, using bold colors and combining them in ways that surprise people. All kinds of materials show up in my creations: paint, spray inks, stamps, vintage items, paper, fabric, etc. I love documenting emotions and everyday moments through art, art journals, and scrapbook pages. I am the author of *Art of Layers*, and I have a line of licensed design stencils with The Crafter's Workshop™. My artwork has also been published in several magazines and idea books, including *Artful Blogging*; *Somerset Memories*; *Creating Keepsakes*; *Memory Makers*; *Scrapbooks, ETC.*; and *Scrapbook Trends*.

With a degree in education, teaching comes naturally to me. I have taught classes on altered-art projects and canvases; color theory; mini albums; basic and advanced scrapbooking; beginning, intermediate, and advanced stamping; cards; mixed media; and technique. I encourage you—in both art and life—to live boldly, color brightly, and love always.

 TO FIND OUT MORE

Visit **www.rondapalazzari.com**. Connect with Ronda on Pinterest: **@RondaPalazzari**.

MIXED MEDIA
Ronda Palazzari

Ponder Bird Canvas

This mini panel makes for a quick and simple project. Make several for a collection for your yourself or to give away as gifts.

TOOLS & MATERIALS
6" x 6" wooden painting panel
Gesso • Matte medium
Various papers (pattern tissue,
text pages, etc.)
Acrylic paints (various colors)
Paintbrushes • Embossing stylus (optional)
Drawing pencil • Modeling paste
Stencil • Palette knife
Thread (optional)
India ink and calligraphy nib
(optional)

STEP 1 Prepare the panel with gesso. Then, using matte medium, adhere old text, vintage dress patterns, old ledgers, and other various paper items to the background. This gives the mixed media piece a foundation of pattern and texture.

STEP 2 Begin building up the base of the piece with layers of acrylic paint. Light colors are great for backgrounds because they allow the patterns to peek through. I use white and light yellows, with touches of blue around the edges.

STEP 3 While the paint is still wet, add some texture by scratching into the paint, using the bottom of a paintbrush or an embossing stylus. Scribbles, words, or images all look great scratched into the paint, revealing some of the underlying layers of pattern.

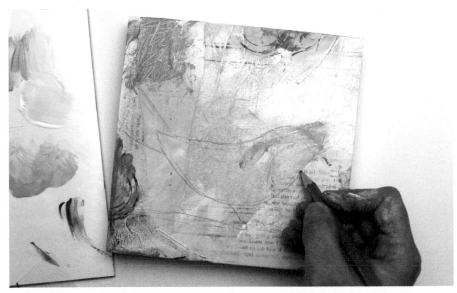

STEP 4 Sketch or trace a bird onto the panel. To create a dynamic image, I place the bird in the bottom two-thirds of the canvas with its tail leading off the left side.

STEP 5 Paint the bird and twig with colors that will pop against your background, using more than one color to give the image depth. I use magenta, reds, and yellows on the bird and paint in short strokes to create a feathered look.

STEP 6 Use stencils with modeling paste to add another layer of texture. I mix green paint with the light modeling paste and scrape it through the stencil, using a palette knife. The green leaves are a great complement to the red bird.

STEP 7 My favorite part of the process is adding in those finishing touches that really complete the piece. For the raised wing, I adhere vintage thread with matte medium to create a unique look. I outline the bird and add other shapes and letters around the panel with india ink and a calligraphy nib.

ARTIST TIP

Three is a good number
in design—the human eye
finds items in threes visually
pleasing. Note that I put
three leaves on my branch
and stamped three times with
my tape dispenser piece.

STEP 8 Found objects, such as the plastic piece in a tape dispenser, are always fun to use. I paint the piece with india ink and stamp the image around the canvas.

STEP 9 You can continue adding embellishments to your mixed media piece if you desire. There are no rules with this art form, and you can use other items you may have around the house to create unique textures or add a special focal point to your piece.

MIXED MEDIA
Ronda Palazzari

Miss Frances Collage

Use paint and scrap papers you have on hand to create a colorful collage worthy of any wall in your home.

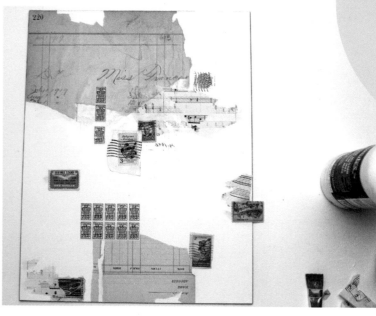

STEP 1 Collage old ledger papers, music sheets, stamps, and other items onto a clayboard canvas, using gel medium. You can use a brayer to help smooth out any bubbles or wrinkles. Rip some of the papers up once they become tacky, leaving a transfer behind. Paint gel medium on top of some of the pieces to create a resist.

STEP 2 Begin adding color to the piece with watercolor crayons, keeping in mind that the colors will eventually be blended. Two complementary colors (red + green, blue + orange, yellow + purple) make brown.

STEP 3 Add oil pastel geometric marks. Then activate the watercolor crayons with water and a large flat brush. Remember to clean your brush as you move around the canvas. The colors turn bold with just a touch of water, and you can begin to see the resist from the gel medium. The oil pastel marks will resist the water and keep their shapes.

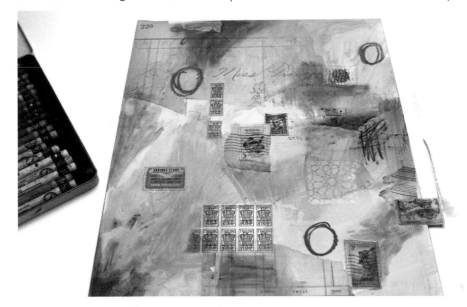

STEP 4 You can go back in and add more colors, filling in empty spots or areas that need a pop of color. Try adding more oil marks in different shades.

STEP 5 Add a little bit of water to some gesso to create a gesso wash. Use a wide flat brush to apply the gesso wash around the canvas, using short strokes and leaving some open areas. The gesso picks up some of the watercolors and blends them a little further, creating a cool effect. Clean the brush between strokes so that the colors don't bleed.

STEP 6 While the gesso is still wet, add some scratches into the wash with an embossing stylus, revealing the colors below. Add more interest to the canvas by scratching into the clayboard with a paper piercer or craft knife.

STEP 7 Make some more marks on the clayboard by dripping liquid acrylics down the surface of the canvas.

STEP 8 Using a marking pencil, draw a black motif on the canvas to pop against the color. Activate the drawing with water to really make it stand out.

STEP 9 Add a few more marks around the canvas, using dashed lines or other geometric shapes. You can add as many marks as you wish before declaring your masterpiece complete.

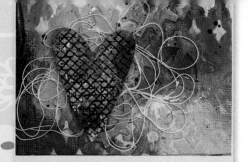

MIXED MEDIA
Ronda Palazzari

Tangled Heart

This colorful mini collage is the perfect pop of texture and vibrancy on a desk, end table, or bookshelf.

TOOLS & MATERIALS
4" x 4" canvas
Gesso • Paintbrushes
Stencil (optional) • Palette knife (optional)
Molding paste (optional)
Acrylic paints (various colors, including white, black, and gray)
Paper towels • Cosmetic sponge
Die cuts • Heart die cut
Stamp of choice • White thread
Matte medium

STEP 1 Paint a thin layer of gesso on the small panel canvas. Add another layer over "gears" or other die cuts to create dimension on the canvas.

STEP 2 To create even more texture and dimension, scrape gesso through a stencil with a palette knife. If you want a more defined look, try using molding paste instead of gesso. Add the gesso or molding paste in random patterns around the canvas.

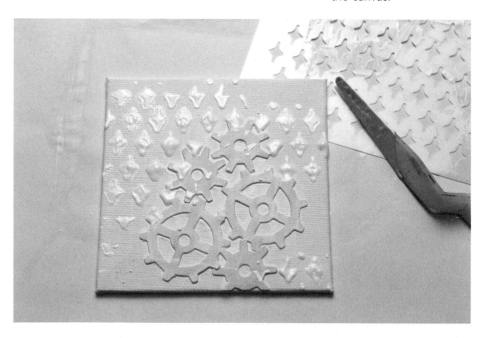

STEP 3 Paint the canvas with acrylic paints. You can layer many colors on top of each other. Try wiping away some of the layers with a paper towel to reveal the layers underneath. Grab two or three colors on your paintbrush to create depth in the paint, and make sure you push the paint into the die cuts.

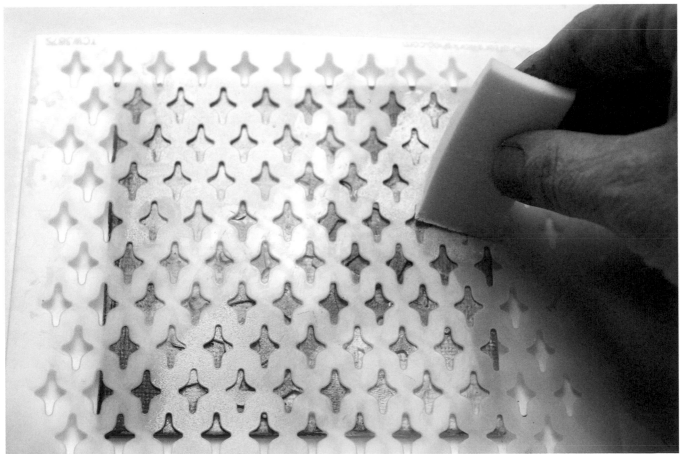

STEP 4 Using the same stencil, add a layer of white paint with a cosmetic sponge in a pouncing motion through the stencil. Again, use a random pattern to create interest and movement.

STEP 5 Die-cut a heart shape and paint it with black, white, and gray paint. Let it dry completely before adding a stamped image on top of the heart.

STEP 6 Next add some black spatters to your canvas—it's amazing how this little touch can finish the look. Mix water with black acrylic paint. Then load a round paintbrush and tap it against your finger to create tiny splatters of paint. Run black paint around the edges of the canvas.

STEP 7 Adhere white thread to the canvas in a swirly mass, using matte medium and a paintbrush. Finish by adhering the heart on top of the thread.

ⓟ **ARTIST TIP**

Display your new mini piece of art on a small easel.

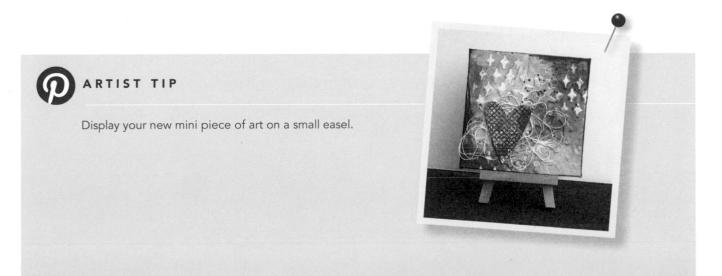

Ideas & Inspiration

Create an inspirational style board! Use these pages to draw, sketch, doodle, brainstorm, and paste photos, ideas, and concepts for original mixed media projects.

Create a Virtual Portfolio or Scrapbook

with Laurie Gatlin & Roy Reynolds

You can create 100 percent original content on Pinterest by uploading images from your own camera or computer. Create a board that functions as a portfolio, scrapbook, or photo album. You can group your photos to share with friends and family or build your online portfolio presence. If you don't want to post your images publicly, create a secret board and invite family members or friends. Note that all members of a group are able to post images and comments.

ILLUSTRATOR ESSENTIALS

WANT TO BE AN ILLUSTRATOR?
YOU'LL NEED THESE...

COFFEE

SNACK FOODS OF WHATEVER VARIETY YOU CAN MUSTER THE ENERGY TO PREPARE.

DRAWING IMPLEMENTS*
*OR FOR THE DEVIENTS, SCISSORS & GLUE

SIGH.

ASPIRIN AND/OR BENZODIAZEPINES

JAR OF TEARS

HARD HAT (METAPHORICAL)

A CREEPING AWARENESS OF YOUR OWN MORTALITY

* JUST KIDDING, COLLAGE ARTISTES!

ILLUSTRATION

Gemma Correll

**ARTIST
PROFILE**

**CREATE A
SELF-PORTRAIT**

**HOW TO
DRAW A CAT**

**ILLUSTRATED
CERAMIC MUG**

" My work is narrative-based,
with a strong emphasis on word
play, humor, observational
journalism, and pugs. "

Artist: Gemma Correll

Hi, I'm Gemma. I am a cartoonist, writer, illustrator, and all-around small person currently based in the United Kingdom. I have qualifications in basic first aid and grade 5 flute, as well as a first-class degree in illustration from the Norwich School of Art and Design (UK). These skills have enabled me to forge a career in freelance illustration and cartooning (and also help you out if you break your finger).

My work is narrative-based, with a strong emphasis on word play, humor, observational journalism, and pugs. I specialize in hand-drawn comics, characters, typography, and pattern. I divide my time between commissioned work, producing illustrations for clients—including *The New York Times*, *Knock Knock*, and Hallmark—and working on personal projects, such as designing and selling my own range of comics, cartoons, and screen-printed tote bags. I also

draw a monthly *Skycats* cartoon for the Emirates Airlines *Open Sky* magazine.

I have exhibited around the world in Asia, Canada, the United States, and Europe and have given presentations about my work at events, including the 2012 Pictoplasma character design conference in Berlin, Germany. In 2010 I was the recipient of a Young Guns 8 Award from the Art Directors Club of New York.

I am the author of *A Cat's Life, A Dog's Life, A Pug's Guide to Etiquette, A Pug's Guide to Dating,* and *What I Wore Today.* My greeting cards and gift range, Pickle Parade, is available from various retailers, including Paperchase and WH Smith.

I chronicle my (mostly) boring life through illlustrated diary entries on my blog and work alongside my trusty sidekick, Mr. Norman Pickles the Pug. My favorite color is turquoise, my star sign is Aquarius, and my favorite word is Albuquerque (in case you were wondering).

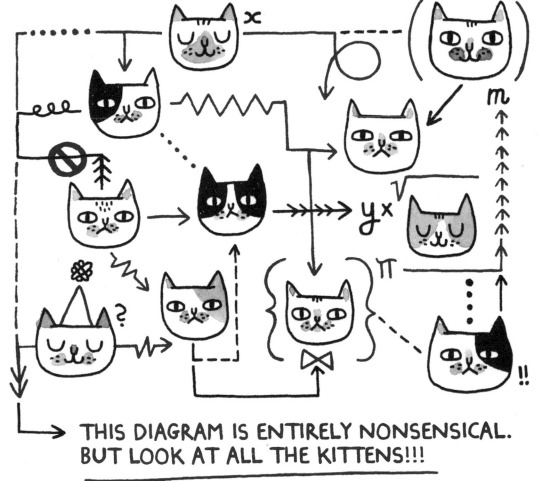

THIS DIAGRAM IS ENTIRELY NONSENSICAL. BUT LOOK AT ALL THE KITTENS!!!

GEMMA CORRELL

TO FIND OUT MORE

Visit **www.gemmacorrell.com**. Connect with Gemma on Pinterest: **@gemmacorrell**.

Create a Self-Portrait

The perfect way to get started in clever illustration is with a self-portrait. After all, what better model than your wonderful, fabulous self?

pens or pencils (whatever you prefer)

a mirror

STEP ONE
Look in the mirror. Go on... take a good look at yourself, young lady/man. What are your most noteworthy features?

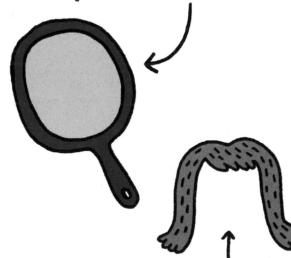

Your hair?

your accessories?

That birthmark in the shape of a three-legged hamster?

STEP TWO
You can draw a very basic face shape with two eyes, a nose, two ears, and a mouth... Y'know, all the usual things.*

+ c :)) →

* Unless your noteworthy feature is your third ear. If it is, I'm really sorry and totally did not mean to offend you.

STEP THREE

How are you feeling today? You can change the facial expression using just the mouth and eyebrows.

Here are a few examples.

Look how simple it is to change the expressions using very basic lines. Try out a few different expressions.

STEP FOUR

Now add to this basic face your noteworthy, extra special, fantastic features.

To make it look more like me, I'll add my glasses.

I should really get a haircut

And now, since I am not bald, here I am with hair.

STEP FIVE

Add some color, if you're into that kind of thing. I'm going to give myself some rosy cheeks, because I like to think of myself as some kind of cartoonist Snow White. (Except instead of dwarves, I have pugs.)

rosy cheeks

cheesy grin

Ta-da! Finished! Your very own cartoon self-portrait.

ILLUSTRATION
Gemma Correll

How to Draw a Cat

Cats are fun to draw. Follow along with the step-by-step process and tweak as needed to replicate your favorite furry feline friend.

Your preferred drawing materials

Real-Life Kitty muse (non-essential, but recommended)

STEP ONE

I start with the face and ears...

Draw in this direction. Try and do it in one continuous Line.

STEP TWO
Next, the tail...

and butt (tee hee)

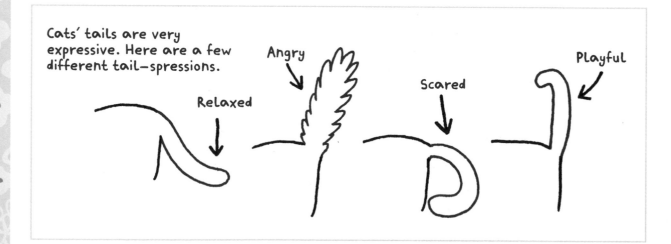

Cats' tails are very expressive. Here are a few different tail-spressions.

Relaxed

Angry

Scared

Playful

STEP THREE
Give the poor cat some legs already!

Don't forget the tiny kitty toes. Aww!

Follow the same basic outline but make your line squiggly for a fluffy cat.

STEP FOUR
Let's draw the face now. Try out some different expressions.

disdainful (default)

shocked

happy

angry

sleepy

guilty

noisy

windy?

STEP FIVE
Add some essential details.

whiskers

jaunty hat

food bowl

fur

expensive toys that he never plays with

snazzy bow tie

ARTIST TIP

Look at some real cats (or just look on the Internet, it's basically made of cats) and try drawing their markings.

You can simplify them to get a good, graphic effect.

... or just make it up!

Illustrated Ceramic Mug

Tired of the same old boring coffee mug you drink from every morning? Spice things up with your own unique, illustrated ceramic mug. Make a bunch to give as gifts... or keep them all to yourself.

White ceramic mug

Pencil (optional)

Ceramic paint pens, or permanent markers (any colors)

Wet wipes

An oven, pre-set to 350*f / 180*c (optional)

STEP ONE
Decide what you're going to draw on the mug. Here are some ideas...

A witty and hilarious slogan

GIVE ME COFFEE OR DIE

Your star sign

A coffee-related pun

I ♥ YOU A LATTE

I'm going to draw a cat with lots of legs because... well, why not?

STEP TWO

Draw your design out on paper first.

You can also pencil the design out on the mug, if you feel like it.

STEP THREE

Start drawing your design on the mug.

Start on the opposite side to your drawing hand so that you don't smudge your artwork as you go around the mug.

Don't worry if you make a mistake—just wipe it clean with a wet wipe while the paint is still wet. (Make sure it's dry before you continue drawing.)

STEP FOUR

If you used paint pens, you can make your mug dishwasher safe by baking it in the oven for 45 minutes at 350*f / 180*c (or whatever your paint pen packaging tells you to do).

While you wait, eat some cookies. You deserve it.

Ideas & Inspiration

Use these pages to illustrate your family and friends, your pet, your dinner, or whatever else your heart desires!

P **Doodling**

Flora Chang

ARTIST PROFILE

DOODLE TOWN

LITTLE INKY MONSTER

PAPER DOLL

> "In my creative journey, I am at the point where I want to draw like a kid again, just simply enjoying the process and not overthinking anything."

Artist:
Flora Chang

My name is Flora Chang. I was born and raised in Taipei, Taiwan. I live in Overland Park, Kansas, and work as a fulltime designer for a greeting card company, where I draw and design children's cards every day at work.

Growing up, I always loved to doodle. I remember drawing all over my textbooks, adding funny outfits or mustaches on photographs of historical figures. My mom was an art teacher, and I remember fondly attending workshops with her because she was always learning from others. To this day, I love taking creative classes and learning new skills.

I moved to San Francisco for graduate school to study graphic design, which landed me my current job as a greeting card designer. I started my blog "Happy Doodle Land" as a place where I share my personal doodles and creations with the world. It was intended to be a playground for me, but as I grew my portfolio I began to receive requests for prints of my artwork. I opened my Etsy shop in 2009, where I sell art prints and other handmade creations.

I love to doodle. I illustrate digitally at work everyday, but my favorite thing to do is sit down with my sketchbook and just doodle by hand. I rarely go anywhere without my sketchbook and a black fine line marker pen. I am crazy about colors, but black-and-white line work has a special place in my heart. I like to fill a whole page with doodles—until I can't fit one more thing—before moving on to a new page. Sometimes I add color to my hand-drawn doodles—mostly red—and sometimes I add pencil lines because I love how it adds a different texture to the drawing. I glean a lot of inspiration from children's art. In my creative journey, I am at the point where I want to draw like a kid again, just simply enjoying the process and not overthinking anything. Organic forms, folk art, vintage children's books, and objects that are weathered with beautiful textures also inspire me.

I feel very humbled and blessed to be able to make a living by drawing and doing what I love. I am really lucky to be able to connect with many creative souls through my blog, my shop, and my Facebook page. It has been a fun ride indeed.

 TO FIND OUT MORE

Visit **www.happydoodleland.com**. Connect with Flora on Pinterest: **@florachang**.

DOODLING
Flora Chang

Doodle Town

I have heard people say that they'd like to doodle more but they struggle with, or are afraid of drawing, characters. If that's you, this doodle prompt is perfect—it's mainly composed of dots, lines, and shapes! This doodle project is very easy and only requires a few colored markers to complete. I use three different colors, but you can use only two, or just black if you just want to create simple line work. As you draw, don't worry about wobbly lines or trying to draw all the shapes perfectly. As a matter of fact, I adore the organic quality of wobbly lines—I think they add charm to a piece. So try to keep your hand relaxed while you doodle, and have fun with it!

TOOLS & MATERIALS
White paper
Fine line marker pens
(black and red)
Light gray felt-tip marker
(optional)

STEP 1 Grab your black fine line marker and start the doodle by drawing a row of various-sized rectangular shapes on top of each other. When you reach the end of the first row, draw a pointy top to cap it off. Then draw another row in the same manner.

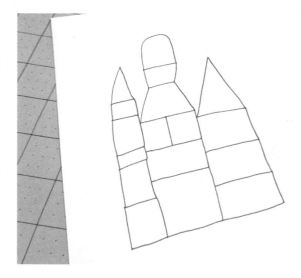

STEP 2 Just like playing with real toy building blocks, continue building your town by drawing various-sized rectangles on top and next to each other. As you draw, try to mix in other shapes, such as triangles or half circles, to make your town more interesting.

STEP 3 Keep drawing stacks of shapes until you have the outline of the whole town.

STEP 4 Now it's time to decorate! Add dots, lines, circles, or other interesting icons to the blocks with your black marker. Pay attention to where you add the details. If you add dots in one block, try to draw something different in the neighboring blocks; the goal is to mix things up. Reserve some blocks for the red details in the next step.

STEP 5 Switch to your red marker and add details inside the remaining empty blocks.

STEP 6 Next fill some of the blocks and design elements with red.

STEP 7 Repeat the process with black. If you want to introduce a third color after this step, reserve some blocks for that.

STEP 8 To finish, I choose to add a third color: a very light gray. You can also use a brighter color if you want it to "pop" more. Notice that I left a few blocks alone without adding any background color; it's good to have some breathing room.

Before you start doodling, test all the colored markers you plan to use on a piece of scrap paper. Lay down some black first; then run the red marker against the black to see if it muddies the red. Test the gray color in the same manner. Pay attention to the edge where the colors meet, and make sure the colors don't bleed into one another. If the colors do muddy each other, try different brands of markers until you find a good combination.

Little Inky Monster

TOOLS & MATERIALS
Watercolor paper
Black ink fountain pen
Pan pastel (pink)
Cotton swab
Small watercolor brush
Cup of clean water

This is a really fun and simple doodle exercise that uses only a few materials. I discovered this technique when I accidentally splashed drinking water over my ink doodle. Yes, the drawing was ruined, but the accident produced a really soft and unexpected inky effect, which I really loved. In this project, we'll put what was originally an accident to good use, and draw a cute monster.

STEP 1 On a piece of watercolor paper, start your monster doodle by drawing the head and body first, using the black fountain pen. I did my line in a zigzag fashion, but you can use clean lines if you prefer.

STEP 2 Add eyes, horns, a nose, and legs to finish the drawing.

STEP 3 Now the fun starts! Dip your small watercolor brush in clean water. Then apply to your monster, starting with the head.

STEP 4 Stay within the lines and touch the inky line work with your wet brush. The black ink will start to spread with the water, creating a fun and soft inky effect.

STEP 5 Continue painting with water until you fill up the whole body. Then let the drawing dry completely.

STEP 6 Once dry, add a few hairs on the forehead with the pen. Brush over them lightly with the wet watercolor brush.

▶ **STEP 7** Dab a little bit of pink pan pastel color with a cotton swab and apply it to the monster's cheeks. Use your finger to even out the color. I love using pan pastel because it produces a soft, glowing effect.

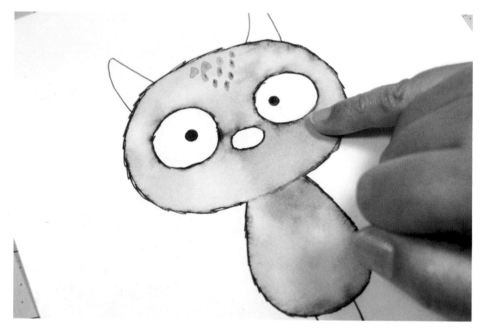

STEP 8 Add a funny face to your monster! Draw a big smile, some teeth, and a few freckles.

You can create lightly inked water to apply to your drawings for extra accent or texture. Draw an ink blob with your black fountain pen on a piece of scratch paper; then use the small watercolor brush to apply water over it.

STEP 9 Add some stripes to the monster's horns, and then apply water to the stripes. Add arms and a few more hairs to the body, and apply some water to the hairs as well. I put some pink pan pastel in the ears and drew a little flower to finish the doodle.

Paper Doll

Playing with paper dolls was one of my favorite childhood activities. I had a big flat pencil case with different partitions to keep my eraser, ruler, pens and other little objects organized. Sometimes I emptied the box and filled each partition with tiny paper furniture and paper people that I made and played house. It was magical for a little kid.

This is a fun project to do, especially with children, and it's very easy. I use a limited color palette for my doll, but you can make yours however you want. If you don't have thick watercolor paper, you can also use the reverse side of a cereal box, as long as the material is study.

TOOLS & MATERIALS
Heavyweight watercolor paper
Red and light pink brush-tip markers
Fine line black marker (permanent)
Scissors
Pencil
Craft knife and cutting mat (optional)
Circle template (optional)

STEP 1 Draw the outline of the doll's hooded cape with the red brush-tip marker on the watercolor paper. Play with the proportion between the head and the body; personally, I love to draw a larger head.

STEP 2 Draw a bow at the neck of the cape, using the fine line black marker.

STEP 3 Switch back to the red marker and color the whole hooded cape.

STEP 4 Use the fine line marker to give your doll hair, eyes, a nose, and a smile.

STEP 5 Add more details to the doll by adding arms, legs, and a scalloped edge along the bottom of her cape.

STEP 6 Give her a pair of red shoes to match her outfit. Then add some blush on her cheeks, using the light pink marker.

STEP 7 Time to construct the paper doll. Use scissors or a craft knife and cutting mat to cut across the bottom of the doll. Then trim along the edges.

STEP 8 Make a base for your doll. I used a circle template because I like my base to have a curved top. Draw the outline of the base and mark the center point. Then cut out the base along the outline and cut along the center mark about halfway through. Make the center cut a little wider to accommodate the thickness of the watercolor paper so it will be easier to connect the doll.

STEP 9 Cut a slit at the bottom of the doll, making sure it's centered. As with the base in step 8, make the slit a little wider to accommodate the thickness of the paper.

STEP 10 Connect the paper doll and the base. Your paper doll is now ready to play!

ARTIST TIP

You can make other characters using the same techniques. Why not make a house and a kitty to join your little doll? Create a whole scene as you wish, and get ready for storytelling time.

Ideas & Inspiration

Use these pages to practice doodles for your doodle town, inky monster, and paper doll. Or fill them with new doodles and ideas!

PINTEREST TIP

Pinterest as a
Marketing Tool

with Laurie Gatlin & Roy Reynolds

Both nonprofit and for-profit organizations proliferate the Pinterest-sphere. Libraries and universities use Pinterest to note new and worthwhile items in collections. Bloggers use Pinterest to draw traffic to their sites—some have gained millions of followers doing so.

Web-entrepreneurs use Pinterest to draw attention to their stores on Etsy or other sites. By building a large group of followers, you have a built-in showcase for your handmade wares. Thinking of starting your own small business? Consider creating a separate Pinterest account to promote your business.